Greetings Cards
to Make and Treasure

SEARCH PRESS

First published in Great Britain 2009

Search Press Limited
Wellwood, North Farm Road,
Tunbridge Wells, Kent TN2 3DR

Based on the following books in the Simple and Stunning
series published by Search Press:

Handmade Art Nouveau Cards by Judy Balchin, 2007
Handmade Oriental Cards by Polly Pinder, 2007
Handmade Celtic Cards by Paula Pascual, 2008
Handmade Clear Stamped Cards by Barbara Gray, 2008
Handmade Fairy Cards by Judy Balchin, 2008
Handmade Paper Pierced Cards by Patricia Wing, 2008
Hand Painted Rustic Cards by Ruth Watkins, 2008
Handmade Victorian Cards by Joanna Sheen, 2008

and on *Joanna Sheen's Paper Lace Greetings Cards*, 2008

Text copyright ©Judy Balchin, Polly Pinder, Paula Pascual,
Barbara Gray, Patricia Wing, Ruth Watkins and Joanna Sheen, 2009

Photographs by Debbie Patterson and Charlotte de la Bédoyère,
Search Press Studios and by Roddy Paine Photographic Studios

Photographs and design copyright © Search Press Ltd. 2009

ISBN: 978-1-84448-394-5

The Publishers and author can accept no responsibility for any
consequences arising from the information, advice or instructions
given in this publication.

Readers are permitted to reproduce any of the items in this book
for their personal use, or for the purposes of selling for charity, free
of charge and without the prior permission of the Publishers. Any
use of the items for commercial purposes is not permitted without
the prior permission of the Publishers.

Suppliers

If you have difficulty in obtaining any of the materials and
equipment mentioned in this book, then please visit the Search
Press website for details of suppliers: www.searchpress.com

Alternatively visit the authors' websites:

Barbara Gray: www.claritystamp.co.uk
Ruth Watkins: wooden-it-be-lovely.com
Joanna Sheen: www.joannasheen.com

Printed in Malaysia

Publisher's note

All the step-by-step photographs in this book feature the
authors demonstrating how to make handmade greetings
cards. No models have been used.

Greetings Cards
to Make and Treasure

Judy Balchin, Barbara Gray,
Paula Pascual, Polly Pinder,
Joanna Sheen, Ruth Watkins
and Patricia Wing

Contents

Materials

At the beginning of each project is a 'you will need' list so that you know exactly what to gather together before making the card. Below are some general guidelines for cardmaking materials, and some more specific advice on what you need for the cards in each section of the book.

Basic materials

There is some basic equipment that is common to most cardmaking such as a **craft knife**, **cutting mat** and **metal ruler** for measuring and cutting card and paper. **Scissors** are also useful of course, and you can buy special craft scissors which will cut a wavy or scalloped edge. Some of the projects in this book also require a **circle cutting system**, although in some cases, **compasses** and **cuticle scissors** can be used instead. Some cardmakers like to use a small **guillotine** for cutting straight edges and trimming cards and borders. **Decoupage snips** are needed for some of the projects in this book. **Craft punches** are used to make some of the cards. A **cocktail stick** and **tweezers** are used for some fine work, and other basics that crop up several times are **pencils**, **ballpoint pens** and **masking tape**. Various types of brush are also required such as **paintbrushes**, **large**, **soft brushes** and **stencil brushes**.

Paper and card

Many different types of paper are required for cardmaking, in fact, gathering together the different types can be half the fun! The projects in this book call for many different types of paper such as: **handmade paper**, **watercolour paper**, various **background papers**, **tissue paper**, **tracing paper**, **photocopier paper** and **vellum**. You will also need various types of card including **pearlescent card**, **glitter card**, **mirror card** and **card blanks**.

Adhesives

These are a vital part of the cardmaker's equipment, and most crafters have their own favourites. Some of the glues used are **strong glue**, **PVA glue** with a fine-tip applicator, **silicone glue** and **spray clear adhesive** (also known as **spray mount**). **Double-sided sticky pads** (sometimes called **3D foam squares**) are useful for cardmaking, as are **double-sided sticky tape** and **low-tack sticky tape**. Some projects require an **adhesive roller** or a **pinpoint roller glue pen**.

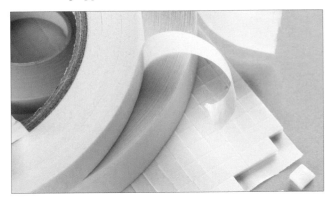

Rubber stamping equipment

Many of the projects use **rubber stamps** and **inkpads**: the specific stamp details and colours are given in the 'you will need' lists at the beginning of each project, but you can of course use your own choice of stamps to personalise your cards. Joanna Sheen recommends using **unmounted stamps** with an **acrylic block** for her Victorian cards. She also uses **baby wipes** to clean up stamps and hands. Barbara Gray's clear stamped cards require the stamps as specified in the projects, and she also recommends a **brayer**, some **chalk inkpads** and an **archival inkpad**, a **make-up sponge** and large **sticky yellow notes** like those found in offices. Some of the projects specify **instant drying inkpads**, **solvent inkpads** or a **watermark inkpad**. You will also need **embossing powder** and a **heat gun** for some of the cards.

Embellishments

Crafters use all kinds of pretty bits and pieces to finish off cards. The projects in this book include **gems, ribbon, gold thread, seed beads, metal embellishments, sequins** and **ultra-fine glitter**. One of the oriental cards uses **netting with a wave pattern**, and another uses **twigs** and **leaves**.

Special materials

As well as the general materials that are common to most cardmaking, you will need specific materials for each section of this book.

Rustic Cards

For the projects in this section you will need **acrylic paints** in burgundy red, cream, pale yellow, green, blue, turquoise and mid-brown, and both round and angular **brushes** in various sizes. Ruth Watkins uses a **ceramic daisy dish** in which to lay out and mix her paints, and adds water to them with a **pipette**. You will also need **waterproof pens** with fine tips, and non-waxed or water-soluble **transfer paper** and a **stylus** or empty ballpoint pen for transferring designs. A fine-tipped, clear **embossing pen** is used with **embossing powder** to create a raised design.

Paper Lace Cards

In this section, Joanna Sheen uses some images and background papers that are printed from special **crafters' CDs**, available from Joanna's website (details at the front of this book). She also uses **laser-cut lace**, a **paper doily** and a **bone folder**.

Paper Pierced Cards

In the projects in this section, Patricia Wing uses **paper piercing templates** and a **pricking tool and mat**. There is also a **rub-on transfer** and a stick to apply it.

Victorian Cards

Here Joanna Sheen uses a **lace patterned backing paper** from a pad, and kitten images for decoupage from a **Victorian themed CD**.

Celtic Cards

For the cards in this section you will need **alcohol inks** with an **applicator** and **blending solution**, and a **cotton bud**. Colour is also applied with **fine fibre-tip pens**, and one card is decorated with **imitation gold leaf**.

Oriental Cards

The Waves and Water card in this section requires glass painting equipment: **glass paints** and a **brush**, **outline paste** and **acetate** to paint on.

Art Nouveau Cards

For the Lilies and Dragonflies card in this section, July Balchin has used a **stencil** with **blending chalks** to create the image and **fixative** to fix it. For the Grapevine Gate Card, you will need **embossing foil**, and **lighter fuel** is used with a **tissue** to rub away colour.

Fairy Cards

One of the cards in this section requires silver **embossing foil** and an **embossing tool** and **vitrail clear gloss glass-painting varnish**; the other one features **polymer clay**, which is worked on a **ceramic tile**, a **rolling pin**, small leaf and flower **cutters**, a **clay shaper** and **baby wipes** for cleaning up.

ART NOUVEAU CARDS

by Judy Balchin

My love affair with the Art Nouveau period has been going on for most of my adult life, so you can imagine my pleasure when I was asked to write this section, combining it with one of my favourite crafts – cardmaking.

The French term 'Art Nouveau' means 'New Art'. It was a wonderful art movement lasting from 1880 to 1915. This short period has left us with a legacy of beautiful artworks and designs which are still used today. The artists and craftsmen of this period used organic and ornamental shapes to produce flowing, intertwining work integrating all aspects of art and design. Simple or complex, the Art Nouveau style is instantly recognisable in its balance and harmony. It arose as a reaction to the Industrial Revolution, the high level of craftsmanship contrasting hugely with the machine-made, mass-produced goods typical of the day.

My biggest challenge in writing this section was to evoke the style and colour of the Art Nouveau period using paper, card and decorative embellishments. It has been a wonderful journey and I have enjoyed every minute of it.

I hope that you find inspiration from the techniques and ideas in this section. Use it as a launching pad for your own card creations and, most importantly, have fun!

Judy

Opposite
A selection of Art Nouveau greetings cards.

Grapevine Gate Card

Metal embossing is the perfect partner for Art Nouveau designs. The unusual gate design gives a sophisticated look to this dramatic card. Coloured foil is embossed with a popular Art Nouveau grapevine design and then aged by removing the colour from the raised areas. Wrapped with ribbon and embellished with jewels, this card is perfect for any special occasion.

1 To make the gate card, measure and score a vertical line 5cm (2in) in from each side of the larger piece of jade card. Use the blunt edge of a scalpel.

2 Fold the flaps in and glue a strip of handmade paper to each flap.

3 Tape the photocopied template to the back of the embossing foil.

YOU WILL NEED

Jade card, one 20 x 20cm (7¾ x 7¾in) and one 10 x 15cm (4 x 6in)

Pale jade handmade paper, two pieces 4 x 19cm (1½ x 7½in)

Template (see page 24)

Blue embossing foil 10 x 15cm (4 x 6in)

Ballpoint pen

Old notepad

Masking tape

Two blue gems

Blue ribbon, 1m (39½in)

Paintbrush with rounded end

Lighter fuel

Tissue

Strong glue

Spray clear adhesive

Pencil

Ruler

Scalpel

4 Working on an old notepad, trace over the design with a ballpoint pen. Press firmly to achieve a good, deep line.

5 Remove the template and work over the design once more to deepen the line.

6 Use the rounded end of a paintbrush to emboss the areas within the leaf, stems and grapes.

7 Turn the foil over. Use a tissue and lighter fuel to rub away the blue relief areas, leaving them silver.

8 Resting your work on a cutting mat, cut out the foil design using a ruler and scalpel.

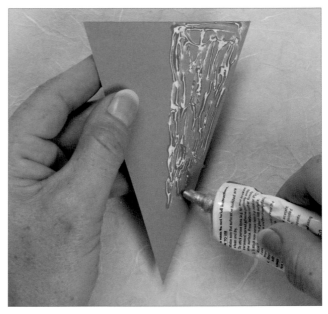

9 Glue the embossed panel to the smaller piece of jade card. Cut round the card using a scalpel and ruler leaving a small border.

10 Turn the panel over and apply strong glue to the right-hand side.

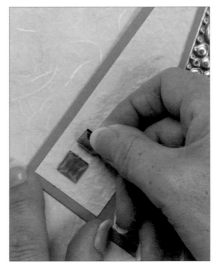

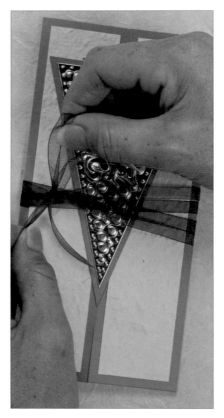

11 With the base card face down and open in front of you, press the panel on to the edge of the right-hand flap.

12 Close the card and decorate with the gems.

13 Wrap the card with ribbon a few times and tie in a bow.

The peacock design shown below is embossed on to silver embossing foil, cut out and backed with pastel floral background paper. It is then decorated with lilac eyelets and brads to create a simple yet effective card. A single embossed peacock feather is used to create a matching gift tag. The templates are provided on page 25.

For the gate card, use the project template and alternative colours and embellishments to create a totally different look. The template is provided on page 24.

The gold embossed roses on the card shown below left are edged with black card and crackled cream paper, then mounted on to gold card to create a sophisticated look. One embossed rose is used to create a matching gift tag. The templates are provided on page 25.

The popular Art Nouveau iris design shown below right is embossed on to turquoise foil. It is then cut out, glued to a gold card panel and embellished with jewels and eyelets. This panel is then glued to a base card decorated with matching handmade paper and finished with a ribbon tied at the fold. The template is provided on page 24.

Lilies and Dragonflies

As nature was the ultimate source book for Art Nouveau artists, this first project is a perfect introduction to their wonderfully organic world. The lily and dragonfly motifs were regularly used in the design of wallpaper, jewellery and furniture. Muted-coloured chalks and background papers give a more aged appearance to the card.

1 Spray the back of the butterfly paper and press it on to the front of the base card.

2 Tape the stencil on to watercolour paper and lightly draw round it with a pencil.

3 Remove the stencil. Use the stencil brush to brush the lower half of the paper with green chalks.

4 Brush the upper half with pale blue chalks.

YOU WILL NEED

Dragonfly and lily stencil

Jade green base card, cut and folded to measure 13 x 16cm (5 x 6¼in)

Heavy watercolour paper, 12 x 15cm (4¾ x 6in)

Butterfly background paper

Blending chalks

Stencil brush

Large soft brush

Two square pink gems

Green ribbon, 50cm (19¾in)

Masking tape

Double-sided sticky pad

Spray adhesive

Ruler

Scalpel

Pencil

Fixative

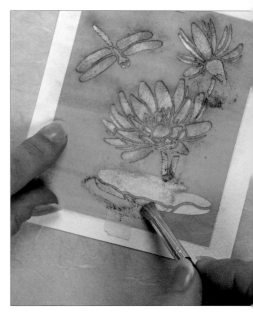

5 Replace the stencil, aligning it with the pencil lines, and attach it with masking tape. Using pink chalk, brush the ends of the dragonfly wings and petals. Shake off the excess chalk.

6 Brush the dragonfly body, wing bases and petal bases with purple chalk.

7 Brush the lily pad with light green chalk, adding dark green chalk to the leaf base and stalks.

8 Remove the stencil and brush away excess chalk dust with a large, soft brush and spray with fixative.

9 Tear round the pencilled line.

10 Lay the card on a piece of scrap paper and brush the torn edge with dark green and dark blue chalks.

11 Spray the back of the watercolour paper with glue and press it on to the base card.

12 Attach a sticky pad to the back of the small piece of green card. Remove the backing paper and press on to the watercolour paper.

14 Wrap the fold with ribbon and tie it in a bow at the top.

13 Glue two gems to the card. Use the blunt side of a scalpel blade to help you position them.

Butterflies were popular images in the Art Nouveau period. This stencilled butterfly is embellished with eyelets and a jewel to add a little sparkle.

This stencilled heart design is embellished with eyelets and a spiral of wire threaded with small key embellishments.

These stylish stencilled angels provide the perfect frame for the central star-studded background paper. A small stencilled star provides the ideal central image for the matching gift tag.

Templates

All the templates required to make the cards in this section are reproduced full size on these pages. You can also use them as a starting point for creating designs of your own. You may decide to vary the scale, using a photocopier, or to apply a different technique to create a card that is unique and personal.

Iris design, page 17

Grapevine Gate Card and matching gift tag, page 12

Peacock design, card and matching gift tag, page 16

Rose design, card and matching gift tag, page 17

ORIENTAL CARDS

by Polly Pinder

The word 'oriental' conjures up so many wonderful images, from the simplicity of formal, understated Japanese designs to the opulence of intricate Chinese brocades. The characters of Far Eastern alphabets are in themselves miniature works of art – they can create exquisite emblems without the addition of any other mark, and can form an intrinsic part of a painting.

Designing and making greetings cards is, in my opinion, equal to making a painting or any other form of high art work. The same creative process is used – the initial excitement when an idea develops into a distinct possibility; then the actual making of the card, bringing all the different components together to form a single image; the wonderful satisfaction of completion, and finally (and this is something not often experienced in the making of a work of art) the grateful appreciation and effusive compliments from the recipient – we hope!

Many of the cards shown here have been copied from or inspired by images from the series of Design Source Books, also published by Search Press. These are simple line drawings which can easily be adapted or developed to suit your own ideas and techniques.

To any committed students of oriental languages: I have done my best to write the characters as accurately as possible and hope that the meaning is correct, but please accept my apologies if I have made conspicuous blunders. Thank you.

Waves and Water

Glass painting is a modern version of the traditional craft of creating stained glass windows, but we use acetate instead of glass and outline paste in place of lead. All of the necessary equipment is available from craft stores.

If you have never used the materials before, try some practice attempts first – the technique is not dissimilar to icing a cake. First secure a piece of acetate on top of the design. Put the smallest dot of paste on to the acetate, then lift the nozzle a little and allow the paste to fall on to the line. Move the tube carefully round the design while continuing to let the paste fall on to the drawing. This way you will have much more control, resulting in a clean line. When the outline has dried, you simply flood the different sections of the design with glass paint.

Outline stickers are a wonderful substitute for paste if you are in a rush or are not quite confident enough to use the paste. There are two examples on pages 32–33.

The Japanese word for wave is 'nami', and it features regularly in traditional and contemporary design and painting. This motif is taken from an heraldic crest.

YOU WILL NEED

Pale turquoise card blank 12 x 12cm (4¾ x 4¾in)

Thin, slightly darker turquoise card 4 x 8cm (1½ x 3¼in)

Sheet of acetate 13 x 13cm (5 x 5in)

Pale blue mulberry tissue paper 13 x 13cm (5 x 5in)

Cardboard 16.5 x 16.5cm (6½ x 6½in)

Tracing paper and two pieces of white paper 13 x 13cm (5 x 5in)

Pencil and ruler

Turquoise and blue glass paint and no. 4 paint brush

Sharp pointed scissors and wave effect craft scissors

Black outline paste with 0.7mm nozzle

Glue stick and low-tack sticky tape

Spray mount and mask

The template for the Waves and Water card, reproduced at actual size.

1 Transfer the design on to one of the pieces of white paper. Place the acetate on top, and use low-tack sticky tape to secure the paper and acetate on to the square of cardboard.

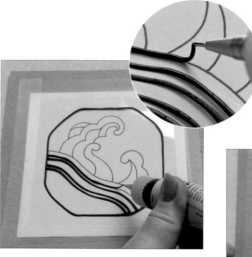

2 Pipe the outer edge of the design first, then the lines of water and finally the waves. Leave it to dry. The inset shows how far above the design the outline nozzle is lifted.

3 Flood each section with glass paint. Take care not to over-fill each area or leave brush marks as a result of too little paint. Leave to dry.

Tip

If you smudge or blob some of the outline paste while piping, leave it to dry and then very gently slice and scrape the excess away with the point of your craft knife.

4 Using the spray mount, stick the mulberry tissue on to the other square of white paper, and then stick the design on to the mulberry tissue.

5 Carefully cut around the edge of the design using the sharp-pointed scissors.

6 Spray the back of the design with spray mount and position the design 12mm (½in) from both the top and the left-hand side of the card blank.

7 Draw four lines 6mm (¼in) apart on the smaller piece of turquoise card. Using the lines as a guide, cut three strips with the wave effect scissors.

8 Turn the strips over and attach them across the bottom right-hand corner of the card using the glue stick.

9 When they are dry, use the sharp-pointed scissors to trim the waves flush with the card.

On formal occasions, Japanese families used to wear their own particular emblems. Over the centuries, many of these crests have evolved, some becoming simplified and others more complex; but they all retain the elegance typical of Japanese design. The gift tag (shown on page 28) takes the simplest elements of the design and positions them within the same shape as the card emblems.

Butterflies Fluttering By

Green and gold always work well together. Here I used outline stickers pressed on to acetate. I then painted the butterflies on the back of the acetate to avoid staining the gold sticker. The dark green handmade tissue paper has fine lengths of gold threaded through it. A circle cutter was used to make the gift tag, which was the inner section taken from the circle of the card.

Perfect Peony

This marble effect was achieved by spreading glass paint on the acetate, allowing it to partially dry and then pressing another piece of acetate on top and immediately peeling it off. After piping and painting, the peony was glued on to white paper, cut out and then stuck on to the marbled acetate. Outline stickers were used for the border. The template is on page 40.

Silver Pagoda

What good fortune to find these large and small pagodas in the form of outline stickers. They were stuck on to acetate, flooded with glass paint and then painted on the back with opaque white glass paint. This prevents the colour from being visually absorbed by the black background. The little yellow symbol means 'luck'.

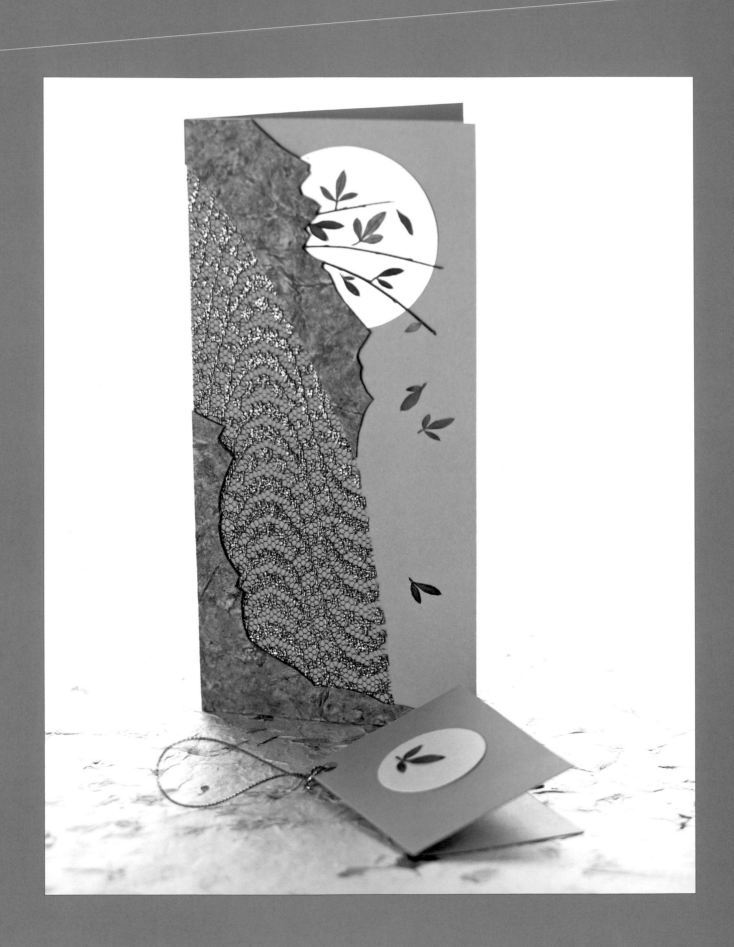

The Moon Beyond the Leaves

Collage: a picture made from scrap paper and other odds and ends; any work put together from assembled fragments. These are dictionary definitions, so really, with collage, anything goes. There are many books on the subject of oriental painting, so you could choose one of the pictures that appeals to you, and then transform it by using any bits and pieces to represent the content or subject of the painting.

The Japanese artist Hiroshige (1797–1858) is a perfect example of an artist whose work can easily be developed using collage. One that I love, *The Moon Beyond the Leaves*, was the inspiration for this card. The title appealed just as much as the subject. I have used pressed leaves, but if you do not have any, you can simply cut some from one of the many lovely handmade papers available.

YOU WILL NEED

Blue card blank 10 x 21cm (4 x 8¼in)

White pearlescent card 8 x 8cm (3 x 3in)

Netting with wave-like pattern 10 x 23cm (4 x 9in)

Handmade textured paper 13 x 15cm (5 x 6in)

Three fine twigs and several small leaves

Tracing paper and pencil

Double-sided sticky tape and sticky tape

Sharp-pointed scissors, craft knife and cutting mat

Compasses and cuticle scissors or circle cutter

White scrap card for the rock and waterfall templates

White paper, 10 x 23cm (4 x 9in)

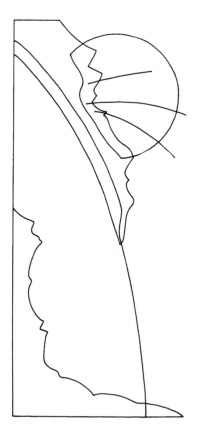

The template for The Moon Beyond the Leaves *card, reproduced at half of the actual size. You will need to photocopy this template at 200 per cent for the correct size.*

1 Transfer all the rock patterns on to card, cut them out and draw round the shapes on to the textured handmade paper. Cut each shape out with the sharp-pointed scissors; you may find it easier to use a craft knife.

2 Transfer the waterfall pattern on to a piece of paper 10 x 23cm (4 x 9in). Pin the netting to the paper and use the sharp-pointed scissors to cut round the pattern.

3 Use a circle cutter to cut the moon out of the pearlescent card, then cut a segment off as shown above.

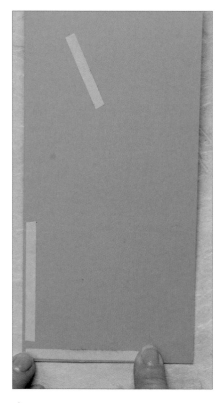

4 Place strips of double-sided sticky tape on to the blue card to secure the netting. Position the strips as shown so that they will be under the rock pieces.

5 Stick the moon in position using double-sided sticky tape.

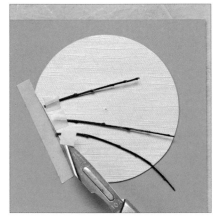

6 Use double-sided sticky tape to attach three twigs across the moon, but do not remove the backing yet. There will be a pinhole in the centre of the moon, so remember to cover it when positioning the leaves.

7 Place the waterfall netting, securing it on the double-sided sticky tape.

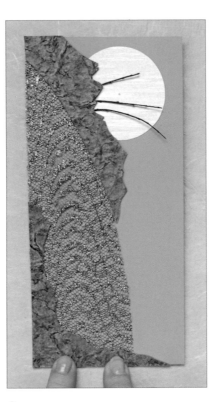

8 Remove the backing from the double-sided sticky tape securing the twigs. Put double-sided sticky tape on the back of the rocks and position them. Make sure the edges line up neatly with the edges of the card.

9 Sort through your leaves and position them on the branches. I find double-sided sticky tape the cleanest method of sticking small items; it is also preferable when gluing dried items. Position two or three leaves floating down by the waterfall to finish.

This is such a simple card to make. The silver and black net represents a waterfall; the rocks are cut from a random-textured handmade paper and the bits of twig are from the garden.

Copper Cockerel

The cockerel is one of the signs of the Chinese zodiac and features in many designs. Here I have used some gorgeous hairy knitting wool for the tail feathers and real feathers for the back and wings. The breast is a lovely embossed paper made from recycled papers and the head and feet are crinkled foil. The little beady eye is, of course, a little black bead. The Chinese symbol is a charm to ensure prosperity and long life. The template is on page 41.

Girl in Gold Kimono

The kimono was originally an informal undergarment of the lower classes in Japan. Over time it developed into a costly outer garment and much importance was attached to its style and the quality, design and width of the fabric. Here I have used stiff ribbon for the kimono, ordinary ribbon for the obi (sash) and gold coloured wire for the hairpins. Everything is stuck on to a little model (see page 40) using double-sided sticky tape.

Golden Dragon

The dragon symbolises Chinese culture; it is king of the animal world and a force for good, protecting man from evil and all malevolent spirits. This glorious fabric was an off-cut that I frayed along each edge – the gift tag is the dragon's tail. The Chinese characters mean 'dragon' and are made from the little waste bits left behind when using outline stickers. The gold centres of the pink holographic flowers in the opposite corner are also dots left behind from sheets of outline stickers. The gold surrounding the orange disc is called 'soft drape feather garland' and the eyes are squares of gold holographic paper stuck on to squares of black card. The template is on page 41.

Templates

All of the templates on these pages are reproduced full size.

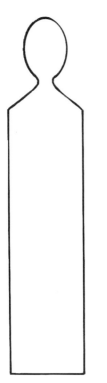

The model for the Girl in Gold Kimono card on page 38, lower left.

The template for the Perfect Peony *card on page 32, lower left.*

The template for the Copper Cockerel card on page 38, top right.

The template for the Golden Dragon card on page 39.

CELTIC CARDS

by Paula Pascual

I couldn't say when it all started, but my fascination with all things Celtic – whether it be design, symbolism, music, history or art – goes back a long way, to when I was a child on the Spanish island of Mallorca. The intrinsic beauty of the Celts is eternal, and goes beyond the barriers of time. Being able to combine it with my biggest craft passion, papercrafting, is a fantastic opportunity for me.

When I am teaching or demonstrating cardmaking, people often ask me to share my ideas on how to make cards for the men in their life. I tried to keep this in mind when I was designing the cards for this section, and therefore included a number of cards with a more masculine appeal.

In the project on page 50 I have provided a template from the book *Celtic Designs* by Courtney Davis, published in the *Design Source Book* series by Search Press/Gill & Macmillan. This book, together with *Celtic Knotwork Designs* by Elaine Hill, *Celtic Borders and Motifs* by Lesley Davis and *The Complete Book of Celtic Designs*, all published by Search Press/Gill & Macmillan, represent a rich source of designs, patterns and inspiration.

The best thing I can say to you is this: have fun experimenting with all the techniques and ideas in this book, and I hope they will inspire you to create beautiful Celtic designs of your own.

Opposite
A selection of Celtic greetings cards.

Celtic Circle

This design uses different rubber stamps to create a beautiful aperture card. I have shown you how to cut out the circular aperture yourself using a circle cutting system, but ready-made circular aperture cards are available. Use good quality felt-tip pens to colour the image, and gold embossing powders to create the raised gold patterns. You will find a stamp positioner extremely useful for this project, to position the gold border accurately.

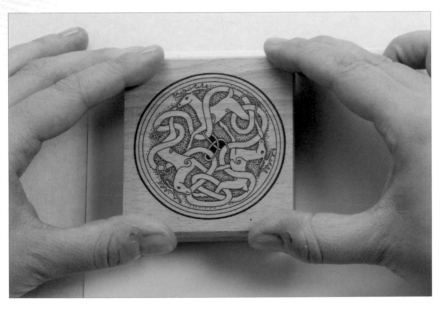

1 Apply embossing ink to the animal design rubber stamp, and stamp the image on to the white card.

YOU WILL NEED

One sheet of A4 white card

Red card blank, 13.5cm (5¼in) square

Circular Celtic rubber stamp with animal design, e.g. Heritage Rubber Stamp Co., Celt4XLS14

Circular Celtic border rubber stamp, e.g. Heritage Rubber Stamp Co., Celt6XLS3

Small Celtic spiral rubber stamp, e.g. Heritage Rubber Stamp Co., CeltLS6

Watermark inkpad

Black inkpad

Gold embossing powder

Heat gun

Red, blue and green fine fibre-tip pens

Stamp positioner

Circle cutting system

Cutting mat

Double-sided adhesive tape

2 Cover the image in gold embossing powder.

3 Tip the excess powder back into the pot. Use a heat gun to heat the image. Hold the gun approximately 10cm (4in) from the surface and stop heating as soon as the embossing powder melts and becomes shiny.

4 Colour in the three animals and the border using the red, blue and green felt-tip pens. Put this to one side and allow to dry.

5 Use the stamp positioner to position the circular border on the card accurately. First, align the acrylic sheet supplied with the stamp positioner with the L-shape. Then apply the black inkpad to the rubber stamp and transfer the image to the acrylic sheet, positioning the wooden block so that it, too, is aligned with the L-shape.

6 Place the inked acrylic sheet on top of the red card. Position the circular design accurately by eye.

7 Align the L-shape with the acrylic sheet as before, holding the acrylic sheet in position on the card.

8 Holding the L-shape in place, remove the acrylic sheet.

9 Ink the circular border stamp with embossing ink and apply the image to the card, aligning the wooden block with the L-shape as before.

10 Emboss the image using gold embossing powder (see steps 2 and 3).

11 Open out the card and, working on a cutting mat, use the circle cutting system to cut out an aperture within the border, just slightly larger than the circular image you made earlier.

12 Stamp the small spiral design randomly over the front of the card using the watermark inkpad.

13 Cut out the circular image and attach it to the inside of the card using double-sided tape, aligning it accurately with the aperture.

For the turquoise card below I first stamped and embossed the image on to white card using a rubber stamp from the Heritage Rubber Stamp Co., Celt3XLS13, and then coloured it in with a high quality felt-tip pen, highlighting certain areas. For the background I used a background script rubber stamp (Heritage Rubber Stamp Co., Celt6XLS1). I used a watermark inkpad for a subtle pattern. I then wrapped the background in gold and turquoise organza ribbon before attaching the central motif.

The tall, thin card on the right uses a stamped image of a labyrinth (Blade Rubber Stamps, 'Chartres') – a highly symbolic image often seen in Celtic and later Christian art. The background was stamped using a watermark inkpad, and the same design was stamped and embossed three times on to white card, cut out and glued on to the front of the card.

There is no reason why you cannot use pretty pastel colours with Celtic motifs. Below left I have stamped and embossed the image (Heritage Rubber Stamp Co., Celt4XLS5) on to white card and coloured it to match the colours of the card. I also added ribbon to give the card more texture.

Animal motifs are amongst the most popular Celtic images, and on the card shown below right I have combined a striking animal design (Heritage Rubber Stamp Co., Celt4XLS2) with red, gold and green to create a strong image that is perfect for Christmas.

Spiral of Light

When it comes to adding impact to your cards, there is nothing as fun and as amazing as alcohol inks. These beautiful inks allow you to colour any non-porous surface, and will dry instantly. The inks blend together even when dry, allowing you continually to add different amounts of various colours until the desired effect is achieved. The addition of tiny patches of imitation gold leaf makes it glimmer and sparkle as it catches the light, enhancing the jewel-like quality of this card.

Template for the design, actual size. (Reproduced from Celtic Designs *by Courtney Davis)*

YOU WILL NEED

Dark green pearlescent card blank, 10.5cm (4¼in) square

One piece of black card, at least 9cm (3½in) square

One piece of gold metallic card, at least 9cm (3½in) square

One sheet of A4 transparency paper

One sheet of A4 photocopier paper

One sheet of scrap paper

Alcohol inks in various golds and greens

Alcohol ink applicator

Alcohol ink blending solution

Cotton bud

Pinpoint roller glue pen

Small pieces of imitation gold leaf

Adhesive roller

PVA glue in a fine-tip applicator

Scissors or craft knife

1 Make several copies of the design on an A4 sheet of transparency paper. Do this by first copying the design several times on to a sheet of white photocopier paper, and then copying this on to transparency paper.

2 Choose the best quality image, cut it out and place it face down on a piece of scrap paper. Place drops of alcohol ink in various shades of gold and green so that they blend together on the pad.

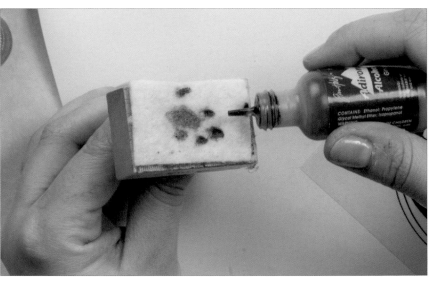

3 Stamp firmly over the back of the design. Build up several layers of colour, turning the design over regularly and varying the inks used to achieve the required effect.

4 Remove the ink from the tiny circles on the design using alcohol ink blending solution applied with a cotton bud.

5 Apply a thin coat of low-tack glue to each circle using a pinpoint roller glue pen.

6 Lay small pieces of imitation gold leaf over each circle.

8 Trim the black card so that it is approximately 1cm (½in) smaller all round than the card blank, and cut a piece of gold metallic card just slightly smaller than this. Mount the two pieces of card on the card blank using the adhesive roller.

7 Turn the design face up and trim carefully around the outside using a sharp pair of scissors. Retain the outer black line.

9 Attach the design to the front of the card using PVA glue applied to the dark areas of the design only.

To create the intricate pattern on the card below is really easy. Make two copies of your chosen design on acetate and then apply alcohol inks to both of them. Remove the inks from the circles. Once dried, trim the designs to size and attach them on top of glitter paper so that it shows through the gaps.

For the card on the right, I matched the colours of the patterned paper with the alcohol inks, and applied transparent glitter glue to highlight the pattern on the main motif. After the glitter glue had dried (it takes a while for glitter glue to dry on acetate), I trimmed around the motif and attached it to the card.

The design below left is very similar to the project; the difference is that the clear gaps are left clear so that the texture of the card underneath shows through. Finish the card by stamping an image in each corner using gold ink.

For a card with a difference, position the main motif over the top edge of the card, as on the design shown below right. Just make sure there is an envelope large enough for the entire card! Stamp the frame (Heritage Rubber Stamp Co., Celt4XLS3) on to turquoise card and trim around it, glue a piece of silver paper on the back and then attach the complete motif to the card. Apply alcohol inks to the peacock and attach it to the inside of the frame.

PAPER PIERCED CARDS

by Patricia Wing

In this section you will find some of my favourite papercraft techniques, with paper piercing used to enhance the main design. I hope you will feel that all the different techniques work well together.

As a child I remember having fun with transfers, so you can imagine my delight when a huge array of fantastic designs became available to cardmakers. The rub-on transfers I have used will give your cards a really professional finish.

The Embroidered Creation card on page 58 features paper piercing, embroidery on paper, sewing on beads and punching, so you can see how the various techniques can be combined in one design.

Have a lovely time paper piercing and making the cards in this section.

Pat Wing

Opposite
These cards illustrate the designs that can be created when combining paper piercing with other cardmaking techniques.

Embroidered Creation

It is always worth every minute when you are making a special card for a treasured friend. In this spectacular square design, embroidery in gold thread sets off the large brass embellishment in the centre and purple beads and punched vellum shapes complete a plush and precious look. It will not take you long to learn how to embroider the panel edges or to sew beads on to the pierced scrolls, but the effect is striking.

1 Using masking tape, fix the pricking template on to a piece of ivory pastel paper. Pierce the scalloped outer border design using a pricking tool and mat.

2 Draw round the edge of the template with a pencil.

YOU WILL NEED

Ivory card blank 144 x 144mm (5¾ x 5¾in)

Two sheets of purple vellum

Gold thread and needle

Pricking template Pro502

Ivory pastel paper, 160 x 160mm (6¼ x 6¼in)

Purple seed beads

Five 3mm (⅛in) faceted gems

Metal embellishment, 35mm (1⅜in) in diameter

Decorative square punch, 25mm (1in)

Pricking tool and mat

PVA glue with fine applicator

Masking tape

Double-sided tape

Pencil and ruler

Fine scissors

Low-tack sticky tape

Craft knife and cutting mat

Tweezers

3D foam pads

  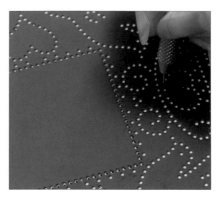

3 Leaving the template in place, pierce the large scroll lightly and the heart design more deeply at the top and bottom of the design.

4 Pierce deeply around the inner square of the design.

5 Remove the template from the paper and turn it ninety degrees. Replace the template on the paper, using the pencilled edge as a guide. Pierce the scroll and heart designs on either side of the design again.

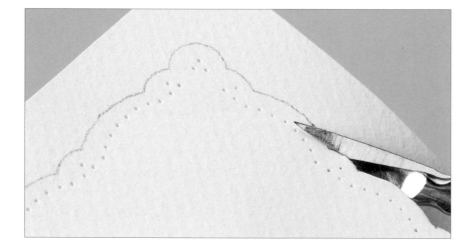

6 Remove the template and cut round the pencil line using fine scissors.

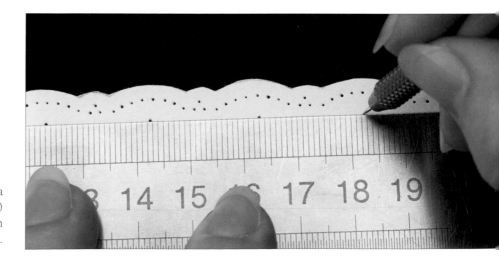

7 On a pricking mat, pierce a hole approximately 5mm (¼in) down from the centre of each scallop. Use a ruler to help you.

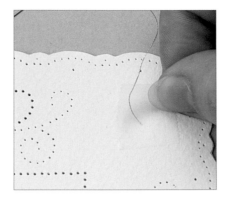

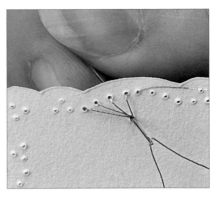

8 Thread a needle with gold thread. At the back of the pricked piece, stick the end of the thread to the paper using low-tack sticky tape.

9 Take the needle through to the front of the piece, coming out of hole 1 of a scallop shape.

10 Go down through the central hole and come up in hole 2. Continue, going down the central hole and up through each of the scallop holes in turn. Repeat for all the scallop shapes.

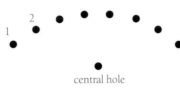

central hole

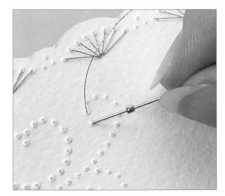

11 Start to stitch the purple seed beads on to the scrolls using back stitch. Come up through hole 2, thread on a bead and go down hole 1.

12 Come up through hole 3, thread on a bead and go down hole 2. Continue in this way until all the scroll is decorated with beads.

13 Mount the stitched card on to purple vellum using double-sided tape and trim the vellum, leaving a narrow border as shown.

14 Mount the stitched card on to the front of the ivory card blank using double-sided tape.

15 Punch four square motifs from purple vellum.

16 Place tiny dots of PVA glue on the back of the vellum punched pieces and use tweezers to stick them in each corner of the main card.

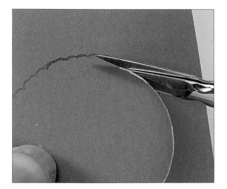

17 Draw round the brass embellishment on a piece of purple vellum. Cut out the circle.

18 Stick the vellum in the centre of the pierced square using 3D foam pads.

19 Use PVA glue to stick the brass embellishment on top of the vellum circle.

20 Glue a gem in the centre of the embellishment and also in the centre of each pierced heart.

Love Token

Pink embroidery frames this pink and cream card. The central gold heart appears to be suspended from a string of tiny pearls, and piercing completes the delicate decoration. The corner piercing is from template EF8015 and the circle is from template Pro0536.

Embroidered Bookmark

Pierced designs from template no. 4.050.366 combined with simple embroidery and silk ribbons make a subtle bookmark that will be a lovely reminder of the giver.

Wedding Card

Embroidered candles and ornate piercing from template no. 5.050.332 surround this brass embellishment and lily decoration.

Embroidered Fan

The fan (template EF8017) is made from paper with a scalloped edge (from template Pro0536) and beads for the spokes. It is decorated with gold embroidery, a leaf bead and gems and surrounded by an embossed frame and corners.

Fairy Princess

A rub-on transfer makes the perfect centrepiece for this fairy card. Daisy shapes punched from yellow vellum surround the fairy, and some are cut up to create her wonderful flowery skirt. Paper pierced flower patterns make a pretty frame and gems and beads add a sparkle to the fairytale scene. The central oval is raised from the main card to add another dimension.

The template for the oval.

YOU WILL NEED

Cream card blank, 135 x 180mm (5³/₈ x 7¹/₈in)

Glistening green vellum

Two pieces of ivory pastel paper, 118 x 160mm (4⁵/₈ x 6¹/₄in)

Yellow vellum

Pricking template Pro540

Rub-on transfer TIP-691 and stick

Daisy punches, 10mm (³/₈in), 15mm (⁵/₈in) and 25mm (1in)

Four 4mm (³/₁₆in) topaz gems

Seven 2mm (¹/₁₂in) topaz gems

Five 2mm (¹/₁₂in) green gems

Gold seed beads

3D foam pads

Double-sided tape

Masking tape

Scalloped scissors

Fine scissors

PVA glue with fine applicator

Pricking tool and mat

Cocktail stick

Tweezers

Craft knife and cutting mat

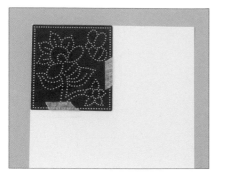

1 Attach the pricking template to a corner of one of the pieces of ivory pastel paper using masking tape.

2 On the pricking mat, pierce the flower and the two large petals. Repeat for the other three corners.

3 Mount the pierced piece on to green vellum using double-sided tape and trim, leaving a narrow border. Mount this on to the card blank.

4 Transfer the oval template on to the second piece of ivory pastel paper and cut out the oval using fine scissors.

5 Mount the oval on to green vellum using double-sided tape and use scalloped scissors to cut a border round the oval.

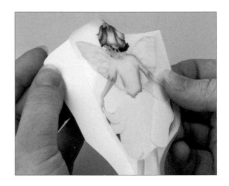

6 Cut the rub-on transfer from the sheet and remove the paper backing.

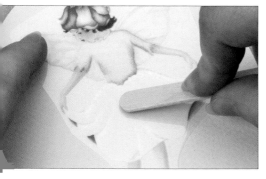

7 Place the design in the centre of the oval and rub firmly using the stick provided.

8 Carefully remove the plastic top sheet.

9 Use the smallest punch to punch twelve daisies from yellow vellum.

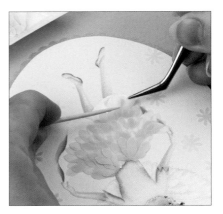

10 Punch a selection of medium and large daisies from yellow vellum and cut them into quarters.

11 Use PVA glue and a cocktail stick to glue the daisies around the fairy design, using the finished card on page 66 as a guide.

12 Glue the petals on from the top down to fill the fairy's skirt. Use a cocktail stick and tweezers to help you.

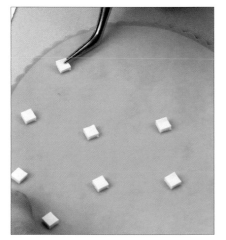

13 Attach 3D foam pads to the back of the oval and peel off the backing.

14 Attach the oval to the centre of the card blank.

15 Stick on the beads and gems using the finished card on page 66 as a guide. The gold seed beads go within the scallops around the oval; the larger topaz gems go in the centres of the pricked flowers and the smaller ones in the centres of the daisies; the five green gems make a belt for the fairy.

Rose Posies

The rose rub-on transfers on this card are surrounded by beads, embossing and paper piercing designs (from template no. 4.050.350). Two shades of purple vellum are used to complement the transfers.

Paper Roses

Six yellow roses and six amber gems decorate this pretty green bookmark. The pricking is from template no. 4.050.356.

Violet Cameo

The central rub-on transfer is raised here to create the effect of a cameo. It is surrounded by smaller rub-on transfers and a Victorian piercing design from templates FR6401 and 3006.

Flowers and Gems

Paper piercing from template no. 4.050.350 creates the perfect decoration around the violet rub-on transfers, beads and gems that adorn this card. The lines within the circle are from template no. 4.050.349.

CLEAR STAMPED CARDS

by Barbara Gray

The art of stamping is, I am told, the most popular and fastest-growing pastime in the world of crafting. During the past twenty years, it has evolved into a sophisticated art form, and using clear stamps opens up countless creative doors, because you can see right through to the surface you are stamping on to align the images perfectly.

Over the years that I have been designing clear stamps, I have developed many ways to use them, and this section will feature some of my tips and techniques which can only be performed with clear stamps.

You can spend a mint on accessories and supplies (if you haven't already!), but all you really need is a stamp, an inkpad, some paper and a quiet half-hour to start. When you first begin, I recommend that you just try playing with your stamp. Try not to judge your first work against the projects shown here: I spent many hours on them, and that was after fifteen years of practice! Just relax and enjoy the art. Skill comes with experience, but fun can be had along the way.

I hope that the projects motivate you to your own works of art, and when you have mastered the techniques in this section, why not borrow one of my recipes and add some spice of your own?

Remember, it is about the journey, not the destination. Good luck!

Reflections

I developed the technique used here when working with a brayer. Everybody who has seen this card loves it, so this has become a favourite technique of mine. Rainbow pads work beautifully here. Never worry that a tree is not green or that the water may not be blue. This is artwork, not a photograph!

YOU WILL NEED

Clear stamps: daydreamer, grass, moonshadow

Dye-based stained glass rainbow inkpad

A4 dark blue card

A5 satin-finish white card

Scrap paper

Brayer

Large sticky yellow notes

Double-sided sticky tape

Craft knife, cutting mat and metal-edged ruler

Masking tape

Pencil

1 Run masking tape round three sides of the satin-finish card, right to the edges. Run a fourth strip along the bottom edge, offset by 1½cm (¾in).

2 Ink the daydreamer stamp on the stained glass rainbow inkpad. Lay it down on the table and roll the brayer over the inked stamp to pick up the image on the brayer.

3 Roll the image on the brayer down on to the card, making sure that the base of the tree is in the centre and the tip of the tree is nearest to the offset end.

4 Turn the card through one hundred and eighty degrees and ink up the daydreamer stamp in the same area of the rainbow inkpad. Align the base of the stamp image with the brayed reflection image already on the card.

Tip

It is much easier to line up a clear stamp than a brayer, so position the brayer image on your card first, then the clear stamp.

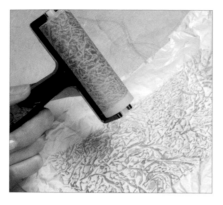

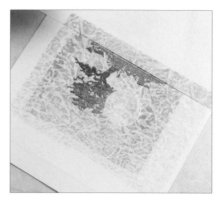

5 Draw two 2.5cm (1in) circles on a sticky note so there is an adhesive area on the back. Cut them out and place one on the right of the tree, and one on the right of the tree's reflection.

6 Crumple some scrap paper and unfurl it. Ink the brayer on the rainbow pad and roll it over the unfurled paper, creating a marbled effect on your brayer.

7 Place some scrap paper over the top half of the satin card, and roll the brayer once over the exposed half, making sure that the red ink is at the top of the water.

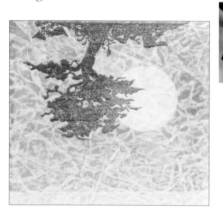

8 Remove the circle mask and lightly roll the brayer over the exposed half again to change the colour of the moon's reflection.

9 Remove the scrap paper and re-ink the brayer. Roll it across some scrap paper at an angle to remove some of the red ink, then roll it across the top half of the artwork, making sure that the faded part is at the bottom of the island. Remove the moon mask.

10 Ink the grass stamp in the green-blue area of the rainbow pad and stamp fairly randomly across the top edge of the picture so different parts of the stamp create a foliage effect.

11 Mirror the foliage effect at the bottom by blotting the stamp before pressing it on to the card.

12 Ink the moonshadow stamp across the red area of the inkpad, blot it and carefully stamp over the moon in the sky, looking through the stamp to get the placement correct.

13 Allow the ink to dry, then remove the masking tape. Use a craft knife and ruler to trim the card down so the picture has a 1cm (½in) border all round the edges.

14 Use the larger offcut of card to make a strip 2.5 x 11cm (1 x 4½in). Ink it with a marbled effect in the same way as the lake.

15 Make a dark blue card and attach the artwork and marbled strip with double-sided sticky tape to finish.

The Willow Lady

Using an alternative central stamp makes for a strikingly different finished piece.

The Ice Skater
Lightly sponging along the reflection line gives the illusion of ice instead of water.

Gone Fishing
The lad fishing is actually an addition to the landscape stamp. Use a brayer to place his reflection first, then stamp him in pace. You can then add the landscape around him.

Grids

Grid cards are a joy to create, and the positioning of images is paramount so clear stamps are a must. There are a few basic guidelines: silhouette stamps work best; place the central image first and work outwards; try to avoid overlapping images, and use contrasting colours in neighbouring sections when shading.

YOU WILL NEED

Clear stamps: kissing, hanging vine, small grass, Eiffel tower, camelia, sprig, music score, dancer, piano, vine, fobwatch, Fifi, fern, snob, dippy-toe lady

A5 satin-finish white card

A4 orange card

A4 scrap paper

Craft knife and ruler

Niagara mist chalk inkpad

Persimmon chalk inkpad

Dye-based black archival inkpad

Make-up sponge

Masking tape

Double-sided sticky tape

1 Use masking tape to make a frame round the satin-finish card, then use two more strips laid across at right angles to each other as shown.

2 Use the dippy-toe lady stamp with the black archival inkpad to stamp on a piece of scrap paper. Cut the image out and place it at the corner of the two extra strips of masking tape.

3 Lay another two strips of masking tape on the other sides of the mask.

4 Remove the mask, pinch a make-up sponge into a mushroom shape and use the Persimmon and Niagara mist inks to add colour to the central section.

5 Use the dippy-toe lady stamp with black archival ink to stamp over the chalked area.

6 Remove all of the inner masking tape, then place two new strips to isolate the top right corner as shown.

7 Colour the area with the chalk inkpads, then use the kissing stamp with archival black ink to stamp an image.

8 Use parts of the hanging vine and small grass stamps to add interest to the top of the area.

9 Allow the ink to dry, remove the horizontal strip of tape and lay down two new strips to isolate the right-hand section as shown.

10 Colour with the chalk inkpads, then stamp the area with the Eiffel tower and camelia stamps. Use scrap paper to protect completed areas when using larger stamps.

11 Remove the horizontal masking tape once the ink is dry, then mask off the lower right corner and chalk it as before. Ink and blot the sprig stamp, then ink and use it unblotted over the top for a dense foliage effect.

12 Repeat the process on the lower central part, masking the area, chalking and stamping with the music score and dancer stamp.

13 Repeat the process with the piano and sprig stamps on the lower left area.

14 Use the vine and fobwatch stamps to complete the left-hand section.

15 Use the Fifi stamp, together with the fern stamp to complete the upper left section.

16 Complete the grid by using the snob and small grass stamps at the top, then remove all of the masking tape.

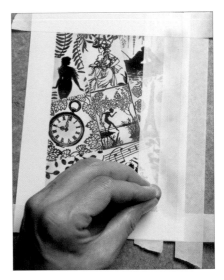

17 Mask off a narrow section on the right-hand side and decorate with the chalk inkpads.

18 Remove the masking tape and use the craft knife and ruler to trim the artwork to size, leaving a ½cm (¼in) border all round.

19 Mount the finished artwork on an orange card using double-sided tape.

Geisha in Red

*This variation uses just one colour in the background.
Here, the central image is not just a single stamp; it is
a miniature section just like the neighbouring areas.*

Africa

You can see here how independent sections can be randomly made to form a medley of African scenes.

Pinch an Inch

Independent fragments of Erté fashion images are built on each other to conjure a mood and a style. The measuring tape adds a subtle humorous twist.

VICTORIAN CARDS

by Joanna Sheen

My love for all things crafty has spanned my entire lifetime and is, I feel, the happiest hobby on earth. My specific interest is in looking back to times and standards of craftsmanship gone by. I love the gentleness of the Victorian era and the belief, so embodied in Victorian crafts, that 'if it's worth doing, it's worth doing well'. I see no point in making a card that looks as though you have not bothered to take care with your craft. I make quick cards all the time, but you should always take that extra moment or two to make sure you really are giving something that can be treasured.

I hope you will take inspiration from the projects in this section and will enjoy applying them to your card making. You can follow a card exactly and make a replica, or you can use papers or embellishments that you have in your workbox that will make your card unique.

The cards manufactured in those days had so many small touches of extra care – and I try to do likewise with my cards. Pretty inserts add a little something to a card. If you have scraps left, why not decorate the back of the card with a strip of toning paper and a craft sticker.

Many of the cards shown here feature toppers or backing papers printed out on a home inkjet printer from one of my Victorian-themed CDs. These are an invaluable source of images and ideas, but if you do not have a computer, there are lots of ready-printed decoupage sheets, backing papers and photographs available.

I hope you have many hours of fun both reading and using this section of the book and I hope you find the Victorian style as addictive as I do!

Joanna Sheen

Opposite
A selection of Victorian style greetings cards.

Decoupage Kitten

This beautiful kitten image is made into a pretty card using decoupage techniques that give the finished project an interesting three-dimensional effect. The images I used are printed from a Victorian-themed CD set and the lace paper is from a ready-printed pad, but you could choose your own alternatives.

YOU WILL NEED

Guillotine

Two sheets of A4 brown card

One sheet of lace paper

Decoupage kitten images

Double-sided tape

Silicone glue

Craft knife

Tweezers

Decoupage snips

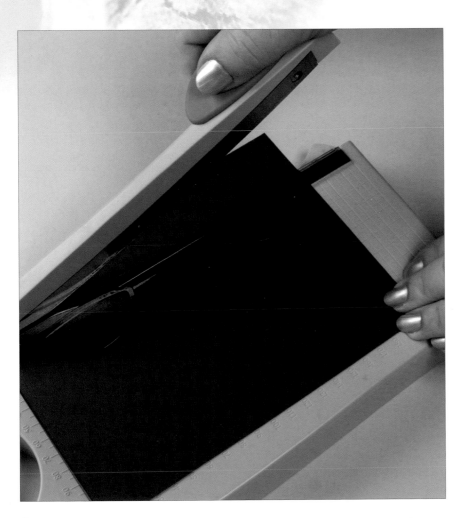

1 Score and fold an A4 piece of brown card in half. Use a guillotine to trim the folded card to 20 x 14.7cm (7⅞ x 5⅞in). Also cut a piece of the same brown card to 16.5 x 11.4cm (6½ x 4½in).

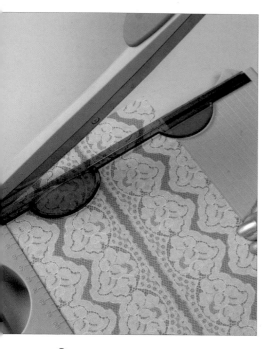

2 Cut the lace paper to 19 x 13.7cm (7½ x 5⅜in).

3 Take the four kitten images and cut them out as shown, using decoupage snips.

4 Apply double-sided tape to the backs of the lace paper and the piece of brown card.

5 Peel off the backing from the double-sided tape and mount the lace paper and the brown card on the main card. Apply double-sided tape to the full kitten image and mount this on top.

6 Apply silicone glue to the back of the next kitten image (top right of step 3) and mount this on the card. Next, apply silicone glue to the back of the next image (bottom left of step 3). Use a craft knife to help you apply blobs of silicone glue. Always clean your craft knife immediately when using it with silicone glue, or use a cocktail stick instead.

7 Apply silicone glue to the backs of the final pieces and place these on the card using tweezers. Leave them to dry for at least half an hour and preferably overnight before putting the card in the post.

Exotic Birds

Birds are popular with both men and women, so this makes an excellent card for a whole range of people. The birds are decoupaged and the picture mounted on several layers of cool blue marbled papers. The black edges bring out the colours beautifully and add contrast to the overall design.

He's Bigger Than Me!

This delightful vintage image of two dogs makes a wonderful focal point and shows how effectively a Victorian image can be decoupaged. The colour toning of the marbled papers and gold and brown card gives a very satisfying result.

Oriental Elegance

Cards with an oriental theme have long been a favourite of mine and indeed this theme runs through many original Victorian designs. Here stamping and paper weaving are combined to make an intricate and subtle card that will give real pleasure to the recipient. The papers come from a blue and white ready-printed pad to complement the stamped image.

1 Stick the bamboo design rubber stamp on to the acrylic block. Leave the stamp lying flat and tap the midnight blue inkpad on to it to ink it.

2 Take the white card blank and place scrap paper inside to protect the aperture area. Stamp the card randomly as shown.

YOU WILL NEED

Midnight blue solvent inkpad

Bamboo design rubber stamp

Acrylic block for stamping

Ginger jar design rubber stamp

Scrap paper

White aperture three-fold card blank, 13.5 x 24.7cm (5¼ x 9¾in)

Two sheets of white card

Instant drying majestic blue pigment inkpad

Decoupage snips

Guillotine

Three different printed blue patterned sheets

Double-sided tape

Tweezers

Silicone glue

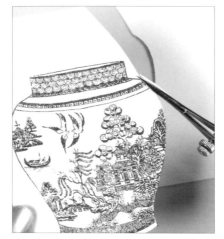

3 Ink the ginger jar stamp with the instant drying majestic blue pigment inkpad and stamp the design on to a white sheet of card.

4 Cut out the ginger jar design using decoupage snips.

5 Use the guillotine to cut 1cm (3/8in) wide strips from the three different printed sheets.

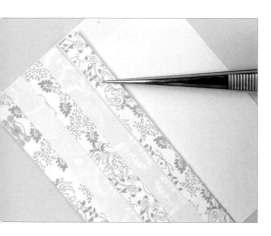

6 Cut a sheet of white card to 9 x 11cm (3½ x 4¼in). Apply a strip of double-sided tape at the top and peel off the backing. Choose strips from two of the patterned papers and use tweezers to stick them alternately across the piece of card.

7 Take strips from the third patterned paper and weave them in and out of the first strips, going under, over, under, over and so on. Leave a strip's width between each.

8 Turn the woven artwork over and apply double-sided tape to the edges of the back. Peel off the backing and use tweezers to fold over the strips to secure them.

9 Apply double-sided tape to the back of the completed woven artwork. Place the artwork behind the aperture of the three-fold card blank as shown. Then fold over the flap so that it sticks to the woven artwork in the right position.

10 Open up the flap again with the woven artwork in place. Apply double-sided tape around the edges of the flap and peel off the backing. Fold over the flap again so that it sticks to the back of the aperture flap.

11 Apply silicone glue to the back of the ginger jar and place it on the card.

Brushing Her Hair

This wonderful image of a small girl brushing her hair is mounted on a background of woven papers with sunflowers and lace mixed together and photo corners have been added for emphasis.

Marbled Cat

The cat image is so strong that it is enough merely to stamp it in sepia without further colouring. The picture is mounted on a card decorated with woven paper strips of warm-coloured marbled papers.

FAIRY CARDS

by Judy Balchin

I have literally been 'away with the fairies' while writing this section and have enjoyed every magical minute of it. The end of every day has found me covered in glitter and usually sporting a few gold and silver sequins as I wander round my local supermarket. This has naturally raised a few comments amongst my friends and family. So at last, here are my lovely fairy projects.

You will be invited to meet my magical friends as you work on the projects in this section: Frost Fairy is beginning to stamp her tiny icy foot – have a go at some enchanted foil embossing! Fun Fairy is dying to be created from colourful polymer clay, and do not forget to visit their friends on the variations pages after each project.

The fairies have all faithfully promised to cast their tiny spells as you work. I hope that by the time you have finished making the cards in the book you too will be away with the fairies... and be proud of it! Have fun,

Opposite
A small selection of Fairy cards.

Frost Fairy

Set this Frost Fairy free! Metal embossing is a wonderfully creative craft and very easy to do. Silver embossing foil and sparkling glitter are used to evoke her icy world. She is backed with starry background paper and strewn with gold stars to complete her enchanted theme.

YOU WILL NEED

Blue base card measuring 12 x 17cm (4¾ x 6¾in) when folded

Star background paper 11 x 16cm (4⁴⁄₁₂ x 6½in)

Grey card 9 x 14cm (3½ x 5½in)

Silver embossing foil 11 x 16cm (4⁴⁄₁₂ x 6½in)

Vitrail clear gloss glass-painting varnish

Small gold sequin stars

Pale blue ultra-fine glitter

Old ballpoint pen

Old scissors

Pad of paper

Paintbrush and large soft paintbrush

Crafter's glue

Strong clear glue

Scrap paper

Masking tape

The template for the Frost Fairy card, reproduced at actual size.

The template for the Frost Fairy gift tag, reproduced at actual size.

1   Use crafter's glue to attach the star background paper to the base card and the grey card panel on top.

2   Place the foil, face down, on to a pad of paper and tape the template on top with masking tape.

3   Use a ballpoint pen to trace over the design, pressing firmly.

Tip
All the embossing work is done on the back of the foil. Turn the foil over to the front now and again to check that you have not missed any of the lines.

4   Remove the template and trace over the lines once more to deepen the embossed line.

5   Cut out the design with scissors.

6   Apply strong glue to the back and press it on to the grey card panel, smoothing it flat with your fingers.

Tip
Shake the excess glitter on to the scrap paper, then fold the paper and pour the excess glitter back into the pot.

7   Paint the background areas generously with varnish.

8   Working over a piece of scrap paper, sprinkle glitter over the wet varnish.

9   Use a large soft brush to remove excess glitter (see inset), then decorate the glitter background with stars, attaching them with crafter's glue.

The Frost Fairy is now ready to fly off into her frozen world.

The templates for the Heart Fairy and tag shown below. The templates are three-quarters of the actual size. You will need to photocopy them at 133 per cent.

Heart Fairy

Watch this silver fairy twinkle as she flies across the pink glitter card. The vibrancy is reflected in the choice of colours used for the base card, background paper and ribbon, giving this card a modern fun twist. Embossed silver mushrooms are used for the matching gift tag.

Templates for the Midnight Fairy and the Golden Fairy cards below, shown at three-quarters of actual size. You will need to photocopy them at 133 per cent.

Golden Fairy

Using the same techniques as for the project, gold foil and silver glitter are used to create this card. The fairy is backed with star background paper and decorated with small gold sequins. The mushroom gift tag uses the same materials.

Midnight Fairy

This gleaming gold embossed fairy flashes across her starlit sky in a haze of dark blue glitter.

Fun Fairy

Polymer clay is great fun to use. Fun Fairy cried out to be created with bright colours and glittery wings and here she is! Make sure that you clean your rolling pin and hands between each clay colour so that you do not contaminate them. Working on a ceramic tile means that, once created, she can be slipped easily into the oven for baking.

1 Working on a white tile, roll out a small amount of white glitter clay, and use the leaf cutter to cut two leaf shapes for the wings.

Tip

Make sure that you keep your hands and equipment clean at all times. Use baby wipes to clean your hands and roller between colours.

YOU WILL NEED

Orange base card measuring 11 x 14cm (4⁴/₁₂ x 5¹/₂in) when folded in half

Patterned glitter card 10 x 13cm (4 x 5¹/₄in)

Yellow card 4.5 x 9cm (1³/₄ x 3¹/₂in)

Polymer clay: white with glitter, flesh coloured, mandarin orange and lime green

White ceramic tile

Rolling pin

Small leaf and flower cutters

Scroll-patterned rubber stamp: Penny Black 2636K

Dot-patterned rubber stamp: Hero Arts LL848 (part of an assorted patterns pack)

Embossing tool

Clay shaper

Double-sided sticky pads

Strong clear glue

Scalpel

Ruler

Baby wipes

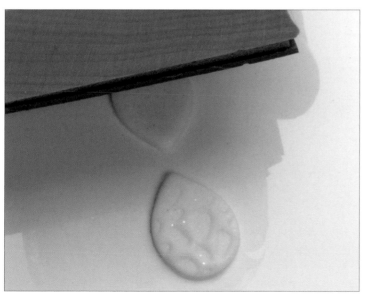

2 Stamp the wings with a dot-patterned rubber stamp.

Opposite:
The fun little mushrooms on the tag are easy to make using the same techniques as for the card itself.

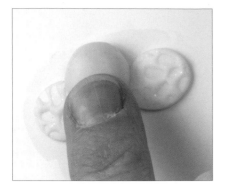

3 Roll a 1cm (⅜in) diameter ball of flesh coloured clay. Flatten it slightly and press it between the two wings.

4 Roll a tiny ball of clay for the nose and press it on to the middle of the ball. Use the embossing tool to create the eyes and the mouth.

5 Roll a small sausage of green clay for the body, 1.5cm (½in) thick. Flatten it slightly and cut across the end. Press this under the head.

6 Roll a long thin sausage of flesh-coloured clay. Cut two 2cm (¾in) lengths for the arms and two 3.5cm (1½in) lengths for the legs.

7 Add a small ball of green clay to the end of each leg. Roll the clay to attach the ball.

8 Press the legs into the green body using the clay shaper to help.

9 Press the scroll-patterned rubber stamp on to a 3cm (1¼in) sausage of orange clay. Press this under the body, across the top of the legs to create the skirt.

10 Press the arms into place.

11 Cut eight small orange flowers using the cutter and use the embossing tool to create the flower centres.

12 Press one flower on to each foot, one where the hands meet and arrange the remaining five flowers round the fairy's head. Bake your fairy on the ceramic tile following the manufacturer's instructions.

13 Use strong clear glue to attach the patterned glitter card to the base card and attach the strip of yellow card to the middle with sticky pads.

Tip

It is a good idea to either bake your fairy right away or cover her as soon as you have finished making her. If left uncovered in her soft state, she will attract dust particles.

14 Glue the finished fairy to the yellow card.

Fun Fairy is enchanted with her ladybird surround.

Head Fairy

Just the clay head and wings of the fairy are used in this colourful card. These are pressed on to a cut-out clay flower which is stamped with the swirl motif. Bright, coordinating papers and card are used to surround our flighty friend!

Swooping Fairy

This fairy is having great fun swooping over the front of the card. She is backed with a large flower cut from background paper which is decorated with pastel flower sequins. A spotted pink paper border continues the fun element. The gift tag uses clay toadstools in matching colours as its theme.

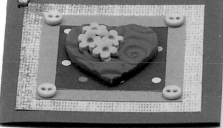

Frivolous Fairy

Vibrantly-coloured clays are used to create this fun fairy. The base card decoration uses panels of card and background papers to reflect the colours of the clay. Small buttons are added for that funky look. The matching gift tag uses a cut out clay heart stamped with the swirl pattern and decorated with small clay flowers.

RUSTIC CARDS

by Ruth Watkins

Welcome to this section on hand painted rustic cards. I am really excited to be given the opportunity to share my love of painting and card making with you. I have always loved creating things right from the time I was a little girl, although I took the scenic route to making my passion my career!

I hope that you enjoy making these cards and get as much pleasure sending them as I did from designing them. My cards feature elements found in the countryside such as sheep, hens and a farmyard cat; butterflies, birds and flowers; rosy red apples; and colourful bunting reminiscent of a village fête. The secret to achieving the fresh country look is to build gentle washes of colour and then enhance with a waterproof pen.

I love bringing each card to life by adding the finishing touches such as stitching and little patchwork hearts – this is definitely my favourite part! The pen is also a great way to cover up any mistakes (or happy accidents, as I call them) by adding a few extra stitches here and there or the odd bumble bee.

Luckily, free-hand drawing skills are not necessary as I have included easy-to-trace templates.

Happy painting!

Ruth Watkins

Opposite
A selection of rustic greetings cards.

Patchwork Apples

I love the beautiful rustic tones used to paint these apples. They look so realistic, you can almost taste them! It is great fun adding all the stitching to the panels and there are more ideas for patchwork-themed cards at the end of this section.

Template, two-thirds actual size. To enlarge to the correct size, increase by fifty per cent.

1 Transfer the design to a piece of watercolour paper measuring 14.5 x 10cm (5¾ x 4in). Use a fine-pointed size 02 black pen and set the ink with a hairdryer.

2 Mix up your colours and begin by laying in the green backgrounds and the leaves, starting with the leaves. Use the tip of a size 4 round brush. Dry the paint with a hairdryer.

3 Paint the cream backgrounds in the lower left-hand panel and the hearts-and-flowers panel, then paint in the jam jars, apple core and blossoms using the same colour. Dry the paint with a hairdryer.

4 Put in the red on the apples in the basket, applying a fairly watery wash first and then adding further washes to build up the colour in the darker areas. Leave tiny bare patches for the highlights.

5 Paint the remaining small areas of red in the same way, and paint in the gingham stripes on the jam jar lids using the tip of the brush.

6 Dampen the backgrounds in the red panels and apply a pale wash of burgundy red. Build up the colour to the desired level with further washes.

7 Continuing with the burgundy red, paint in the hearts, then wet the flower petals and place a dot of colour on their tips. Change to yellow, and paint in the centres of the flowers.

8 Carefully paint the weave and handle of the basket using mid-brown (avoid painting over the black lines). With the same colour, paint in the blossom branches and apple stalks, and lay a light wash of colour on the table in the jam jars panel.

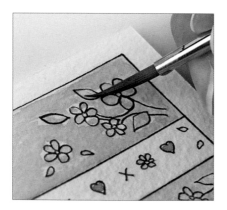

9 Mix a little green and blue together on a tile to create a darker green and strengthen the colour on the lower halves of the leaves. All the background washes are now in place. Dry with a hairdryer.

10 Start to deepen the tones by floating in colour. Beginning with the apples in the basket, use a small angular shading brush to place in the shadows using full-strength paint.

11   Use the same method to deepen the shadows down the left-hand sides of the three apples in a row, then change to the larger angular shading brush and frame the two red panels and the cream panel containing the hearts.

12   In the same way, float green around the edge of the green panel, top left.

13   For the lower right-hand panel, use a darker mix of green by adding a little blue to the green on the tile.

14   Float in a wash of mid-brown around the lower left-hand panel and across the top part of the table in the lower right-hand panel, carefully taking the paint around the jam jars and apples.

15   Lay a gentle float of mid-brown down the left-hand sides of the jars. When the paint has dried, lay a float of burgundy red over the brown placed across the top part of the table.

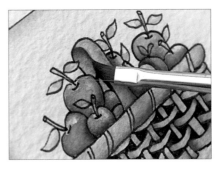

16   Change back to the small angular shading brush and add shadows to the weave of the basket using mid-brown, and down the inside of the handle and along the lower edge of the rim using a burgundy red and mid-brown mix. Dry with a hairdryer.

17   Using a fine, size 1 pen, add the detailing on the leaves, flowers and jam jars, and the stitching. Strengthen any black lines that require it.

18   Trim round the picture with a craft knife and ruler on a cutting mat. Mount the painting on to the dark pink card, and then on to the pale pink card blank.

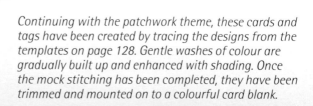

Continuing with the patchwork theme, these cards and tags have been created by tracing the designs from the templates on page 128. Gentle washes of colour are gradually built up and enhanced with shading. Once the mock stitching has been completed, they have been trimmed and mounted on to a colourful card blank.

Here individual pictures with a similar theme or style have been grouped together, and then linked with stitching detail giving a fun and coordinated look. For the matching gift tag just one element has been painted on to a piece of watercolour paper. This has then been trimmed into a tag shape and some ribbon threaded through a small hole created with a hole punch.

Cups and Saucers

One of my favourite pastimes is sharing a cup of tea with friends, so I just had to include this card featuring a stack of old-fashioned cups and saucers! This project uses a soft palette limited to just six colours, and for added dimension I have used an embossing pen, embossing powder and a heat gun to add gold accents on the heart motif and teabag label. So put the kettle on and let's get painting!

Full-size template.

YOU WILL NEED

Acrylic paints: burgundy red, cream, pale yellow, blue, turquoise and mid-brown

Sizes 2, 4 and 8 round brushes with very fine points

0.5cm (¼in) and 0.25cm (⅛in) angular shading brushes

Size 05 brown and sizes 01 and 02 black permanent waterproof pens

Watercolour paper, 10 x 20cm (4 x 8in)

Blue card blank, 10 x 20.5cm (4 x 8¼in)

Fine-tipped, clear embossing pen, gold embossing powder and heat gun

Copy of template and tracing paper

Non-waxed or water-soluble transfer paper and stylus

Daisy dish or ceramic tile, brush basin and pipette

Spare piece of watercolour paper and A4 sheet of printer paper

Paper towel

Hairdryer

Cutting mat and craft knife

Metal ruler and set square (optional)

Double-sided sticky tape

1 Transfer the design to a piece of watercolour paper measuring 10 x 20cm (4 x 8in) using a fine-pointed size 02 black ink pen. Set the ink with a hairdryer. Add the yellow, blue, turquoise, burgundy red and mid-brown background washes, without dampening the paper first, using a size 4 round brush. Make sure each colour is dry before applying the next.

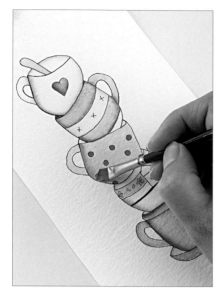

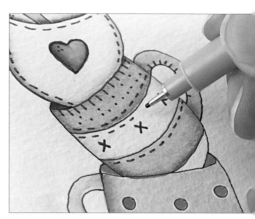

2 Float in colour to create shadows down the left-hand sides and around the tops of the cups, and anywhere else a shadow might fall. Use full-strength paint of the same colour as the background wash on the turquoise and burgundy red cups, mid-brown on the yellow cups, and a mix of turquoise and blue on the turquoise cup.

3 Wet the white background, and use a large, size 8 brush to add random patches of diluted burgundy red, yellow and mid-brown paint. Soften each colour with a damp brush before moving on to the next, and allow the edges to blend naturally on the paper. Leave some areas white.

4 Dry the paint with a hairdryer, and add the detailing and stitching using a size 05 brown ink pen.

5 Outline the circles, flowers and leaves, then change to the size 01 black ink pen and strengthen the black outlines where necessary. Make sure the ink is completely dry before moving on to the next stage.

6 Working on a spare sheet of printer paper creased down the middle, draw around the heart using a fine-tipped, clear embossing pen.

7 Cover the heart in gold embossing powder, tipped straight from the pot.

8 Tip the excess powder on to the A4 sheet and funnel it back into the pot, leaving a gold outline around the heart.

9 Emboss the top part of the tag in the same way, then set the powder using the heat gun. Hold the heat gun approximately 4cm (1½in) above the paper, and move it steadily from side to side to spread the heat evenly. Directly the powder has melted and become shiny, remove the heat.

Tip

You may prefer to hold the paper with a clothes peg to stop your fingers from getting burnt!

10 Draw on the stitching around the heart with the size 05 brown pen.

11 Place the image on a cutting mat, and trim the sides by running a craft knife along the edge of a metal ruler. Leave a border approximately 1cm (½in) wide each side, and 1.5cm (¾in) wide at the top and the bottom. If necessary, make sure the sides are straight using a set square.

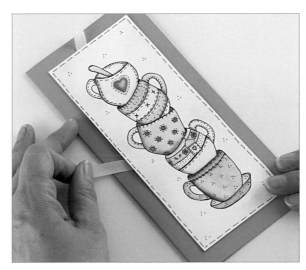

12 Add brown stitching around the outside of the picture, and little groups of three dots on the background.

13 Mount the image on to the blue card blank.

Flowers and butterflies are popular designs as they can be used for all sorts of occasions such as birthdays and anniversaries as well as for thank-you cards. On the butterfly card silver embossing powder has been used to outline the design as well as on the stitching to give a really opulent look. The centres of the flowers and dragonflies on the green card have had gold applied to add interest and texture. The templates for these cards and tags appear on page 129.

On the birthday-themed card, clever use of clear embossing powder enhances the design without being overpowering. Pick out small elements to emboss, such as the bow and the tiny heart on the letter, and once heated the powder will melt to give them a slightly raised and glossy appearance.

The little runaway train has gold embossing powder added to the centres of the wheels and would make a lovely greetings card for a child. The edges of the card have been softened with a round-corner paper punch and then the design has been mounted on to a card which is folded at the top instead of the side. You could use blue instead of pink for a different look. The templates for these cards appear on page 129.

Templates

The templates below are all reproduced two-thirds actual size, unless otherwise stated. To enlarge to the correct size, increase by fifty per cent.

Symbols patchwork card, page 121.

Gardener's delight card and matching patchwork tag, page 121.

Rustic angel card, page 120.

Patchwork flowers, page 120.

Appliquéd apples tag, page 120.

Dragonflies and daisies card, page 126.

Birthday celebration card, page 127.

Runaway train, page 127.

Flower tag, page 126.

Butterfly tag, page 126.

Silver embossed butterfly card, page 126. This template is reproduced at half size. To enlarge to the correct size, increase to 200 per cent.

PAPER LACE CARDS

by Joanna Sheen

Lace is a fabulous ingredient to use in many crafts, and cardmaking is definitely one of them. Adding some lace will soften a design and heighten its femininity. Lace, or lace effects, come in many varieties, and in this section you will find lace made from paper, lace that has been laser cut, lace paper doilies and various ideas for incorporating lace into your designs in different ways.

Fabric lace can be very effective too, but here I have tried to confine the designs to those using only papercraft and cardmaking techniques. I would recommend trying a range of methods, such as stamping and embossing or using ready-made paper lace, and see how lace can add something really special to your cards!

Joanna Sheen

Opposite
A selection of paper lace greetings cards.

Easter Crocuses

This card uses commercially available laser-cut lace, but you could also use real fabric lace to create a similar effect. The soft lavender colour scheme blends beautifully with the colour of the crocuses to make a Spring greeting that would be happily received by anyone at Easter.

YOU WILL NEED

One sheet of A4 purple mirror card

One sheet of A4 pearlescent lilac card

One sheet of mixed-size crocus images, one sheet of matching patterned backing paper and one sheet of matching plain lilac backing paper from the *Cardmaker's Year* CD

A square and two strips of laser-cut lace

Double-sided tape

Silicone glue

Bone folder

Tweezers

Decoupage snips

Scissors

Guillotine

One sheet of A4 cream paper and decorative corner punch for insert (optional)

Cocktail stick

1 Fold the A4 sheet of lilac pearlescent card to create an A5 card blank. Strengthen the crease by firmly running the bone folder along it. Cut a piece of purple mirror card so it is 0.5cm (¼in) smaller all round than the card blank. Attach the mirror card to the front of the card blank using double-sided tape.

2 Cut the piece of lilac backing paper approximately 0.5cm (¼in) smaller all round than the mirror card and attach it to the mirror card using double-sided tape. Cut the crocus-patterned backing paper 0.5cm (¼in) smaller again, and attach this to the top.

3 Cut out one of the smaller crocus images, retaining the dark green border.

4 Trim the square of laser-cut lace so that it fits within the crocus-patterned paper. Apply silicone glue to the back using a cocktail stick and attach it in a diamond shape in the centre of the card. Attach a strip of laser-cut lace above and below it.

5 Apply spots of silicone glue to the back of the crocus image and place it in the centre of the card. Add an insert if you wish.

Lilac Blossom Time

This is one of my favourite images from my Fashion Boutique *CD, and there are numerous designs you can create with it. Here I have paired it with laser-cut lace embellishments and a collection of soft lilac cardstock.*

Vintage Shoes

Long, slim cards are very popular. This is a great format in which to display images of pairs of shoes, but you could also use hats or bags for a similar effect. Use traditionally male images placed in a column down the card for a husband, brother or boyfriend.

Christmas Bells

Christmas is possibly the time when cardmaking is most popular, and how nice it is to have an idea that looks great but isn't too time-consuming to make. This project requires the small-size paper doilies that are intended to go under festive drinks or cups.

YOU WILL NEED

One sheet of A4 red mirror card

One sheet of mixed-size bells and one sheet of matching patterned backing paper from the *Enchanted Christmas* CD

One sheet of A4 forest green card

One small paper doily

Double-sided tape

2mm foam tape

Silicone glue

Bone folder

Tweezers

Decoupage snips

Guillotine

One sheet of A4 cream paper and decorative corner punch for insert (optional)

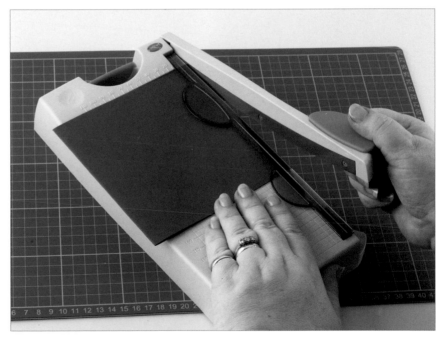

1 Fold the A4 sheet of green card to create an A5 card blank. Strengthen the crease by firmly running the bone folder along it. Trim the card blank so that it is 14.5cm (5¾in) square.

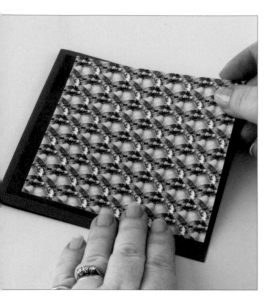

2 Cut the red mirror card so that it is approximately 0.5cm (¼in) smaller all round than the front of the green card blank. Cut the patterned backing paper slightly smaller than this. Attach the mirror card and the patterned paper to the card blank using double-sided tape.

3 Choose one of the bell toppers and cut it out carefully using the decoupage snips.

4 Measure the diameter of the paper doily and cut a square of red mirror card slightly smaller than this. Attach strips of 2mm foam tape to the back of the mirror card square and attach it to the front of the greetings card.

5 Attach the paper doily and the bells to the mirror card using spots of silicone glue for a raised effect.

6 Make an insert for the card if you wish. Add a folded piece of cream paper, slightly smaller than the card. Attach it using a small strip of double-sided tape placed along the fold on the top surface, and round the corners using a decorative corner punch.

Oriental Lace
(below)

On this card the doilies have been folded in half to make fan shapes and slotted in between fans cut from a decorative paper printed from a CD. This design would work well with real miniature fans.

Sepia Bride
(right)

This card uses a large rectangular doily that has been wrapped round the card. It is held on to the card with a ribbon bow rather than glue, which might seep through the paper.

Index